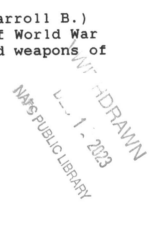

FIGHTING GEAR
OF WORLD WAR I

Equipment and Weapons of the American Doughboy

by C. B. COLBY

Coward-McCann, Inc.   New York

This American Doughboy in his gas mask could easily be the symbol of World War I.

Contents

66-2776

U. S. Army Photos: Pages 4, right; 6; 17; 27; 37. The Smithsonian Institution: Page 16, top. Springfield Armory: Page 26 courtesy of Col. G. B. Jarrett (Ret.), Chief, Ordnance Museum, Aberdeen Proving Ground, Maryland: Pages 22; 24; 30; 31; 34; 36. All others U. S. Signal Corps Photos from the National Archives. Full-color cover transparency courtesy Aberdeen Proving Ground, home of United States Army Ordnance.

World War 1 Fighting Gear

The World War of over four decades ago, still fresh in the memories of many men and women today, was hopefully called "the war to end all wars." Instead it was destined to become the first rather than the last of such global holocausts. Its fighting gear, instead of becoming the last of such equipment, became instead an important chapter in the evolution of our military equipment of today.

This book will answer questions about the kinds of fighting gear used by the American Doughboy of the AEF, the American Expeditionary Forces of 1917–1918, under the leadership of General John J. "Blackjack" Pershing.

Within a year after the entry of America into the war, April 6, 1917, over two million Yanks were fighting in Europe. At first their equipment was a combination of borrowed gear from our Allies, weapons and devices hastily developed and produced here at home, and improvised gadgets produced through American ingenuity in the field to meet the frantic emergencies of the moment.

When we entered the war, America was tragically lacking in almost any kind of weapon or fighting gear. Our firearms, though of fine design, were few in number. We had few military vehicles, and our aircraft industry, in spite of the fact that we had invented the airplane, was almost nonexistent. Our army was small and almost completely inexperienced in combat of any kind, particularly the type of trench warfare being fought in Europe.

In a matter of a few months, however, America's vast energy, her industrial know-how and her ability for teamwork in an emergency began to show results. Supplies, men and fighting gear of every kind began to pour across the Atlantic in ever-increasing tides, while at home everyone joined the war effort with a vengeance.

Those not in the services worked in defense plants or helped tend "war gardens." Boy Scouts and similar organizations sold Liberty Bonds and collected walnut shells for charcoal for gas masks, and every possible industry switched to making more and better equipment for our Doughboys in the trenches.

These historical photographs, many of which have never been published before, will give you an exciting opportunity to look back at the kind of weapons, vehicles, and devices the American fighting man used in World War I.

Many of his first "tools of the trade" were borrowed from our Allies, so they are included also. Some of the equipment cannot be included at all for lack of any suitable photographs, and some that I have included show the ravages of time since the photographs were taken.

With slight exception I have not included aircraft since most of the combat aircraft of the war were of Allied design. What is displayed on the following pages will enable you to compare the equipment of the American fighting man of World War I with that of the GI of World War II, as well as modern equipment for any future national emergency.

The collecting of photographs and the research for this book have been particularly interesting for they brought back memories of those hectic days when the author sold Liberty Bonds, collected walnut shells, and tended his own small war garden in New Hampshire. It also enabled me to work again with many fine people who have been invaluable in the military research for other Colby Books. To them I owe my thanks.

In particular I would like to express my deep appreciation to such people as: Lt. Col. A. S. Williams, Chief, Magazine and Book Branch, Public Information Division, Office of the Chief of Information, Department of the Army; Major Hubert J. Van Kan, Audio-Visual Branch; Mrs. Donna Traxler, Chief, Army Picture Library; Col. G. B. Jarrett (Ret.), Chief, Ordnance Museum, Aberdeen Proving Ground, and Mr. Francis X. Kelly, Deputy Chief, Information Office, Aberdeen Proving Ground. Through their enthusiastic help and courtesy, and that of others, this book was made pleasantly possible.

As you turn the following pages you may find some of the equipment amusing by comparison with military equipment of today, but bear in mind that this was the latest and best of its kind at the time. We owe much to this historic fighting gear of World War I, and to our fathers and/or grandfathers, the Doughboys who used it so courageously and well.

— C. B. COLBY

Uniform of the Doughboy

The soldier of World War I had many problems, and one of them was his uniform. It was of heavy woolen material, usually ill-fitting and anything but wind and water repellent. The spiral puttees consisted of a long strip of woolen fabric wound around his legs from the ankles up and fastened with a tape tucked in at the top. It took time to put them on and they frequently came unwrapped at the worst possible time. Doughboy at left wears full equipment including spare shoes, trench shovel, poncho and blanket roll, overcoat and canteen. Rifle is the model 1917 Enfield .30 caliber. Soldier at right wears same uniform to show front. Note high "dog collar" and "riding breeches" type pants. These laced tightly below the knee to fit under puttees.

Officer Uniforms

The officer's uniform of World War I still featured the tight uncomfortable breeches and the high collar, but sported the famous "Sam Brown belt" as shown here. Many officers spent their own money to have more comfortable uniforms made, and bought leather boots to wear instead of the wrap-around woolen puttees worn by the enlisted men. The officer on the left is the late General John J. "Blackjack" Pershing, Commander of the American Expeditionary Forces, and officer on the right is Admiral Gleaves of the United States Navy. Note Admiral Gleaves' uniform with high collar, no pockets in blouse and old style naval cap.

1st Division Photo Unit

Here is a typical photo unit of World War I, complete with movie camera and "Graflex" box camera, ready to record action of their Division. The photographing of combat and all military activities was the assignment of the U. S. Army Signal Corps, which also handled communications. Model "T" Ford truck in background served as darkroom, transportation and even living quarters in emergency. Movie camera was hand-cranked and reels had to be changed frequently as camera held only comparatively few feet of film. Photo units had tough assignments as taking pictures under fire with unreliable and tricky film and equipment was not only dangerous but frustrating. Many remarkable photographs were taken by such units as this.

First American Wireless in Germany

Historical photo of first AEF (American Expeditionary Forces) wireless station set up in Germany, Dec. 1, 1918, to report American troop occupation of German soil. In those days messages were sent by code rather than voice. Equipment was carried in Signal Corps trailer drawn by light truck. Note bamboo aerial mast left and heavy headset worn by wireless operator. Spare bamboo pole is carried on side of trailer. Range was limited and equipment not always reliable but very important to military maneuvers. This station was established by the 2nd F.S. Battalion, 1st Division, in Kalender Nuhl, Germany.

Artillery Field Telephone

Orders regulating firing of artillery at German lines were transmitted by both wireless and field telephone. This shows an operator using one of the early type field telephones. The wires were strung either along the ground or on poles or trees. These field phones were powered by batteries usually carried in a second box which is used as a seat in this photo. Others were powered by small generators turned by a hand crank, a far cry from the compact Handie-Talkie radios used today.

Gas Masks and Field Phone

During World War I poisonous gas was used by both sides, making use of gas masks a must no matter what the operation. Here is shown a trio of artillerymen using what was called the Tissot Mask, a French Artillery mask of 1917–1918. Note the canister of purifying chemicals carried on the backs of the men. These chemicals neutralized the gas and purified the air which the soldiers breathed via a tube over the left shoulder. Working and fighting while wearing such masks was extremely difficult, but both sides were forced to develop and use them for survival not only from enemy gases but their own. Often a wind shift would carry poisonous gas aimed at the enemy back over the very troops who released it.

"Monsters" of World War I

Here is shown a collection of the various Allied and enemy type gas masks. From left to right: the American mask, the British, French and the German. Only the French covers the entire head, but all used the same sort of air purification chemicals in attempts to make breathing safe. The fiendish gases used during World War I included lewisite and mustard which stayed on the ground for days, making an area dangerous to either side for from three to ten days. Other gases such as phosgene vanished quickly, usually within ten minutes. Gases such as tear gas (used now against criminals and mobs) did not cause permanent injury, but others attacked the lungs or caused huge blisters difficult to heal.

Even the Ladies Wore Masks

All World War I personnel who might encounter poisonous gas were required to take training in the use of the masks and to go through gas chambers to gain confidence in the safety of wearing such masks. Here is shown an Army nurse leaving such a chamber wearing one of the American type masks. These test chambers were filled with comparatively "safe" gases such as tear gas, and an expert was always on hand to assure the trainees of getting through the chamber safely. The carrying pack held not only the purification canister in one side but the mask itself so that it could be carried with the person at all times. During World War II, military personnel were also trained in masks and their uses but there was no evidence that gas was used by either side against enemy troops. Retaliation would have been too terrible had either done so.

Camouflaged Heliograph

Without the convenience and reliability of modern radio and other electronic equipment, the Doughboy of the first World War had to depend upon an assortment of improvised devices. This photo shows a Signal Corps projector lamp camouflaged in a pile of shocks of wheat. This "heliograph" was operated by sighting the light at a receiving station via a sight built into the top of the lens case as shown, and then sending "dots" and "dashes" of light by use of a telegrapher's key on the top of the battery box. This could send messages as far as the light could be seen and by careful aiming, the message could be read only by the receiver aimed at. It also had the advantage of being silent and visual, important during heavy bombardment, and impossible to intercept by radio-listening by the enemy.

Ear-Powered "Radar"

Before the days of radar and other modern means of detecting aircraft, such devices as this were used to locate enemy planes. The sound was picked up in the "dish," concentrated in the center of the hearing unit suspended over it, and then transmitted via tubes to the ears of the observers. It was a sort of giant stethoscope such as used by doctors to hear heartbeats, only in this case it listened for the throb of enemy aircraft motors. By turning the paraboloid surface in its frame the planes could be located and direction of course determined, even if too high to be spotted by eye.

Winged Messengers

Thousands of trained homing pigeons were used during World War I to carry vital messages back to the command posts from the front lines or isolated areas without radio or other contact. Many of them arrived wounded but still carrying their vital messages. Some were decorated for bravery under fire, for their arrival, in spite of wounds, saved many a life when units needed help. (All sorts of tricks were used to confuse the enemy who might listen in on some vital conversations. It is even reported that American Indians in the service were used to speak their native tongues for transmission of important messages.)

Observation Balloon or "Blimp"

Both sides, desperately in need of observation of artillery hits, used such observation balloons as shown here being brought down after an assignment. They were tethered to a ground winch and the observers rode under the bag in a wicker basket from which they could see for miles and report by telephone as to accuracy of barrage fire. The popular name of "Blimp" came from the fact that there were two classes of lighter-than-air-craft. Class A-rigid, which included the dirigibles and zeppelins with rigid metal frames, and class B-limp which denoted the nonrigid and literally "limp" balloons such as these barrage balloons; hence the name "Blimp." Since the balloons were filled with inflammable hydrogen, many were shot down in flames by enemy aircraft as the observers left hurriedly by parachute.

The Enfield Rifle

At the outbreak of World War I our military services did not have a great supply of serviceable rifles. England was experimenting with the Enfield rifle but was to make it in .27 caliber. They switched to the .303 caliber and America made thousands of these for British use before we entered the war. (We were also making our own Springfield as shown on opposite page.) After our entry into the conflict we adopted the Enfield in .30-06 caliber because there was only one armory which could make the Springfield, while so many were already turning out the Enfield. Winchester alone turned out over half a million of these fine rifles. Top photo shows Enfield in side view. Lower photo shows Doughboy using Enfield rifles in 1917 in practice. They are attaching the French Viven Bouchan grenade to grenade launchers on Enfield muzzles.

The Springfield M1903

The famous Springfield rifle, shown here being fitted with a rifle grenade of modern design, was one of the most successful rifles ever designed. Based upon the German Mauser, the Springfield (with some minor changes) has remained the same ever since its first development before World War I. It featured a full wooden stock over the barrel almost to the muzzle, a bolt action and a rather awkward stock butt. It takes five cartridges at once, through the top of the action, in a brass clip, making loading fast and sure. The rifle has a range of over 3,000 yards, and with a more powerful shell and a boat-tailed bullet, over 5,000 yards. It weighs a bit less than nine pounds and is 43 inches long. The Springfield was produced by the hundreds of thousands for use during World War I and it was still in use well into World War II. Marines on Guadalcanal carried this rugged rifle with them into action. It is still used by many sportsmen and can outshoot many an expensive target rifle.

Browning .30 Cal. Machine Gun

If this machine gun with its World War I crew looks like the same gun used in World War II and later, there is good reason, for with a few minor changes it is the same. Invented by John W. Browning of Utah, before the turn of the century, this rapid firing machine gun has seen long service with America's armed forces. It is known as Model 1917 and could fire at the rate of about 450 to 600 rounds per minute. The barrel was cooled by water in the jacket around it, and without water the gun weighed about 33 pounds. Cartridges were fed through the gun in a fabric belt. (Modern models also use a metal-link belt.) It used same cartridges as Springfield rifle.

Hotchkiss Machine Gun

This old photo clearly shows how desperation was the mother of some strange weapons during World War I. Here the light 8 mm. Hotchkiss machine gun is being used as an effective antiaircraft gun by mounting it on an old wagon wheel set on a post. In this way the angle of fire could be almost vertical and the gun could be swung through 360 degrees. This machine gun could fire at a rate of about 450 rounds per minute and had a forged barrel cooled by circular fins (see photo) about the breech.

37 mm. Infantry Cannon

One of the most useful weapons against what was called "points of resistance," such as machine gun nests, small fortified enemy strongholds, etc., was the little French 37 mm. Infantry Cannon. It was mounted on a small tripod and could be moved by two men, one carrying the tripod and the other the gun. It fired a one-pound explosive shell with an effective range of from 1,000 to 2,500 yards. The shell could pierce 7/10-inch armor plate at 2,500 yards with great accuracy. One American crew set a record of firing 36 shots a minute with one of these little cannon. Another famous cannon was the French 75 mm. weapon which was the mainstay of almost all the Allied troops. The 75 mm. was mounted on wheels and had a shield to protect the gun crew. It fired regular, gas and shrapnel shells and could toss them over two miles.

Stokes 3-Inch Mortar

Trench warfare made it imperative that some sort of weapon be devised that would drop explosives into the enemy lines even though well dug in. The trench mortar was the answer as it could toss shells high into the air to drop almost vertically into the deepest trench. Such a mortar could toss all sorts of shells against the enemy — explosive, gas, shrapnel or flares. This photo shows a Stokes crew firing such a weapon. Note projectiles which contain propellant charge as well as warhead on tarpaulin at right. Improved mortars are used by modern armies for same purpose, the dislodging of enemy troops from deep trenches, ravines or behind high fortifications. The Stokes mortar could toss a three-inch projectile about 800 yards.

Newton 6-Inch Mortar

A larger type of mortar was the Newton 6-inch model. This was also used as a trench mortar against strongly fortified positions of the enemy. It could throw various types of shells — explosive, chemical or gas. Note the stout braces, used to hold it in position for firing, on its base. As the recoil of mortars is almost vertical or at least at a sharp angle against the ground itself, no recoil-absorbing mechanism is required as with weapons firing more nearly horizontal. Mortar shells carry their own propellant charges in their bases so that these weapons are really nothing more than strong tubes on a sturdy base. Some fire "finned" projectiles, so the bore is smooth. Others fire finless projectiles, so inside of mortar tube is rifled to give stabilizing spin to projectile. The Newton 6-inch Mortar could throw a sixty-pound projectile about 800 yards.

Our 4.7 Gun

These two photos show the American 4.7 artillery piece being towed (top) and fired in training (lower). Not many of these saw action but they were used in training our artillerymen in handling and firing of similar field pieces. As weight of weapons increased, tractors were rapidly replacing horses and mules for towing heavy equipment, shown in top photo. In lower photo note shells carried in caissons to left of gun.

"Admiral Plunkett's Guns"

This historic photo shows one of the giant weapons improvised to meet a need for heavy guns which could still be mobile. These were giant 14-inch naval guns mounted in special turrets and installed on railway cars. There were four of these made and shipped to France for service. They fired a 14-inch shell weighing about 1,600 pounds for about twenty-five miles. Admiral Plunkett, in charge of project, employed U. S. sailors dressed in army uniforms to service and fire these huge weapons. They did great damage whenever used and were very successful as railway artillery after their conversion at the Baldwin Locomotive Works.

16-Inch Railway Howitzer

Even during the weary months of World War I, research went on to improve our weapons and defenses. Here is a 16-inch railway howitzer crew being trained in the firing of this huge weapon. Note camouflage of gun and railway carriage, the 16-inch shell hanging from its crane behind the open breech of the howitzer, and the powder bags resting in their cradle on the ground. These bags of powder go into the breech behind the projectile and it takes the four men standing by the powder cradle to lift the charge. The range of these railway howitzers was several miles and they were used against heavy fortifications.

Colt .45 Pistol

In contrast to the giant weapon shown on the preceding page, here is the official side arm of our troops, the Colt automatic pistol of .45 caliber. Many thousands of these were made and used during the war and many were still in use by our armed services, even after World War II and Korea. Although they have a husky kick and are not a long-range weapon, they are effective under 100 yards and deadly at closer ranges. Several types of revolvers were also used by our troops, but this weapon was and still is the standard automatic pistol of our services. A seven-round clip fits into the butt and it fires as fast as the trigger is pulled, which makes it a semiautomatic weapon.

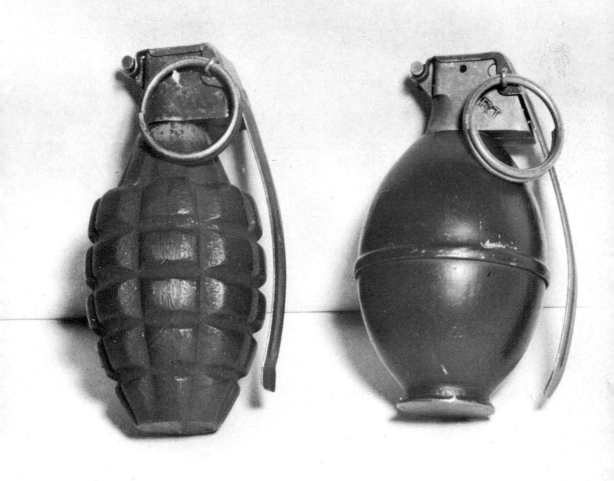

Old and New Hand Grenades

At the ~~left~~ RIGHT is a hand grenade of the type used in World War I and at the right, by comparison, is our modern grenade. During World War I many types of grenades were tried and abandoned. Some were called "potato-mashers" and looked like them, having a short wooden handle attached for throwing. The grooved case of the old grenade at the left made fracture of the case easier when it exploded. The grenade on the right (modern) has a smooth case, is lighter and more powerful. World War I grenades were designed to toss across no man's land into the enemy trenches or machine gun nests. The long metal strip down the side of the grenade kept the grenade from firing as long as the strip was held down. Pulling ring removed safety pin so that when grenade was thrown, this long strip could fly up igniting the short fuse inside. Grenades, like the .45 caliber pistol opposite, are for close-range use. Range of grenade depends upon throwing arm of user.

Grenade Class

This interesting old photo shows a group of American Doughboys receiving instructions in how to use various types of grenades, either thrown by hand or from a grenade launcher attached to the muzzle of a rifle. The French sergeant holds a rifle in his hand with such a launcher attached. On the table before him several types of grenades are displayed. Some are of the familiar old-style serrated case type, but note that two of these World War I grenades are almost identical with the new type adopted by our troops a short time ago. Note in particular the grenade directly in front of the instructor and the one across the table from this one. Compare with new type shown on preceding page. History, even in grenades, seems to repeat itself.

Rifle Grenade Practice

American troops practicing with rifle grenade launchers. Note puffs of smoke out ahead of the dirt bunker where grenades are bursting. The grenade launchers, as you can see, were attached to the muzzles of the rifles (Enfields) and the firing of the piece hurled the grenade many yards. These were used where the range was too long for hand-thrown grenades and no mortars were available for the same use. New and improved grenade launchers are still a popular weapon in use by our troops.

Sidecar-Mounted Hotchkiss

Although the vehicles of World War I, shown on the next few pages, may look amusing, they were designed for deadly business and were the best of their kind for the years of that tragic war. Here, for example, is a light Hotchkiss machine gun mounted on the sidecar of a motorcycle for fast mobility around a battlefield. At the left you see the vehicle with car attached and at right with the car detached and ready for firing, one man firing and the other feeding clips of cartridges into the action. The weapon could also be fired in motion. The sidecar, unlike most such units, has two wheels of its own so that the detached gun carriage could be moved about as a unit without the motorcycle attached.

Colt Machine Gun Cart

This interesting two-wheeled cart was attached to the rear of a motorcycle for fast travel. It could be quickly detached for separate use or fired while in motion. The two-man crew rode on the cart with the gun, one to operate the piece, and the other to serve it with ammunition. This weapon was an air-cooled model of .30 caliber and could fire at the rate of about 400-plus rounds per minute. It was also known as the Colt-Browning gun. Another air-cooled version of this weapon was used on World War I aircraft, firing through the propeller.

"The Tanks Are Coming!"

After months of stalemate when neither side could blast the enemy out of the trenches, desperate measures went forward on both sides to find a means to end the deadlock. On September 15, 1916, a British "solution" rumbled across no man's land to panic the Germans — the first of the great tanks. They had been so secretly built that not even the Allied troops which first saw them knew what they were, except that they were on their side of the struggle. In fact, while they were being built they were said to be a new type of supply "tank" for the troops, to keep their real purpose from being guessed. The name stuck. Those first tanks were slow, easily put out of commission and not too efficient, but they did start an exciting trend in armored vehicles. Photo shows early British tank followed by U. S. infantry using it for protection as they advance toward French town in 1918.

Crawling Fort

Men of the U. S. 27th Division are shown here in training with a British tank which has already seen action with other troops. These tanks were manned by a crew of eight: four gunners, three drivers and an officer. They weighed thirty-two tons and ambled along at a little over three miles an hour. The armament consisted of six Lewis machine guns, two on each side firing from turrets and two firing forward. These could spray trenches with a hail of bullets while the gunners were safe inside the steel hull. Bars over top of this tank were to protect moving treads when tank crawled under heavy barbed wire or from falling trees or debris from crumbled buildings demolished by tank. Doughboys in photo are using British Short Lee-Enfield magazine rifles, caliber .303. They fired ten shots and were called Model 1903. Eight different versions of this sturdy rifle were made during period of use, incorporating minor changes and improvements.

U. S. MK-VIII Tank

This is the tank shown on the cover, the huge MK-VIII, equipped with two six-pound cannon and six .30 caliber machine guns. This great land dreadnought, developed in this country, never saw action due to the signing of the Armistice, November 11, 1918. It was an improvement on Allied heavy tanks. The first British tank, which caused havoc among the Germans in 1916, was named "Mother" and the second one was called "Little Willie." When they began to move across the battlefields of Europe by the hundreds in a single attack, the tide of war began to turn in the favor of the Allies. Germany also built some tanks but only a few. At the end of the war she had only fifty. The first German name for tanks was "Schützengrabenvernichtungsautomobile" which meant "an automobile built for the purpose of destroying trenches dug in the ground." Later it was changed to "Panzerwagon," meaning "armored car"; which must have been a relief even to the Germans.

U. S. 6T Tank

This old photo shows one of the many fast maneuverable American tanks known as the 6T plowing across a trench on its way into action. Many of these were used in the historic Saint-Mihiel drive of 1918. They were lightly armed and armored but could move comparatively quickly and were ideal for cleaning out enemy machine gun nests. Note the shovels lashed to side of turret in case the tank became bogged down in mud. Spare parts and extra equipment were chained to back of top of tank, chain itself to be used to haul tank out of trouble in case of breakdown. Enemy soon found that a hand grenade tossed under tread could put a tank out of commission, or that a wide and deep trench could not be crossed, but with so many put into action by the Allies there were always more coming. They were beginning of armored warfare as we have known it since World War I.

Tank Design Progress

Here are three American tanks on display at the great Aberdeen Proving Ground at Aberdeen, Maryland, home of Army Ordnance. From left to right they are the 3T tank of 1917, the 6T tank of 1917 (preceding page also) and the giant 43T (MK-VIII) tank (cover and page 34) 1918–1919. From this early beginning tanks began to carry heavier armor and armament, increased in speed and range and were much more reliable. The top of the treads became covered for safety against enemy attack, and many new and vastly improved engines were developed. In opposition, greatly improved antitank weapons were devised to counteract these armored monsters. The fantastic Museum at Aberdeen Proving Ground contains thousands of historic war machines, vehicles and weapons, and is visited by military personnel from all over the world to study and examine what others have done in weapons development. The Smithsonian Institution in Washington, D.C., also maintains a fascinating collection of similar weapons and vehicles. If you are ever in our great Capital, do not fail to visit the Smithsonian Institution to see these historic collections.

General "Blackjack" Pershing's Car

Although not exactly "fighting gear," this historic vehicle is worth including in this section of World War I military vehicles. This beautifully preserved Locomobile was the personal vehicle of General John J. Pershing, known affectionately as "Blackjack." It was a special vehicle with many distinctive details designed for his use. Note in particular the double treads on the rear wheels. Spare single-tread front wheels were carried on back of vehicle. Note also special heavy-duty windshield and glass partition between front and rear seats. A real classic in old car preservation!

Ordnance FWD Trucks

This old photo shows an ammunition "train" in France in 1918 making its way up to the front, carrying not only ammunition but all the men who can hang on. These trucks were the U. S. Ordnance FWD (Four-wheel drive) model and had solid rubber tires, which certainly added nothing to the comfort of the passengers and drivers. They were fitted with tarpaulin bows over the top much like the old "covered wagon" of our own pioneer days. Note the kerosene lamps on either side of the radiator and the single headlamp behind the radiator, and the handcrank siren, operated by the driver's left knee. One man rode ahead of the driver in the "cab" to operate the headlamp-spotlight. As awkward and hard riding as these old FWD's were they contributed their very large share to the war effort of World War I.

Field Hospital on the Move

A field hospital of the 13th Ambulance Corps in France prepares to move out to another location. The ambulance in the lead of the caravan, as well as the trucks behind, is covered with brush to help conceal it from enemy planes. It is interesting to note that while the trucks have solid rubber tires, the ambulance is equipped with the softer pneumatic tires for more comfort to the patients inside. The ambulance is an early "GMC" with acetylene gas headlights and kerosene sidelights and taillight. (The following truck appears to be an English vehicle with right-hand drive.) Note racks on ambulance side for three stretchers. In many cases windshields were removed from military vehicles to protect driver from flying glass in case of either near misses from artillery shells or from broken glass due to rough roads. Safety glass was not developed until later. Small photo shows same model ambulance which skidded off road near Lucy, France.

Two Prime Movers

As artillery and other mobile equipment grew heavier, something more than mule power was desperately needed to move it about the battlefields and staging areas behind the lines. Here are two early types of prime movers designed for this work. At the top is a 5-inch wheel-mounted weapon being drawn by a half-track prime mover. Note roller steering wheel, kerosene headlamps, and side curtains in case of rain. Smaller photo shows little ten-ton caterpillar tractor, also with kerosene lamps, used to haul 155 mm. cannon.

"General Mud" vs. Machines

During spring rains and thaws it was said that "General Mud" had taken over, and take over he did, fortunately on both sides of no man's land with equal efficiency. Top photo shows unidentified tractor towing an FWD ammunition truck (same type truck shown on page 38) through thick mud near the Argonne, Varennes, France. Note shells under camouflage net and shelter trenches on hillside beyond. Lower photo shows little 5-ton tractor slogging through mud and snow near Doulaincourt, Haute-Marne. Note camouflage paint. Such caterpillar tractors gradually replaced the rugged army mule on both sides of the conflict.

Railway Troop Transport Car

When you think of the comparative "luxury" in which modern troops travel to and from combat areas it seems hardly possible that troops ever rode from area to area in such railway cars as these. Normally used for freight, horses or mules, these French railway cars did yeoman service hauling troops to the front for many months. Although this particular car is marked "Troops Only" the traditional sign read in French "40 Hommes — 8 Chevaux" meaning "40 men or 8 horses." This was frequently stretched to mean a lot more men than forty. Although we could have supplied rolling stock (cars) for service overseas, the tracks of the French railways would not fit our cars, hence the use of such "freight cars" as this.

Rolling Field Kitchen

During World War I, feeding the men must have been a colossal task without our modern means for food preservation, our modern field kitchens and transportation facilities. The problem was made doubly difficult by lack of vehicles and mechanized equipment for such things as bread mixing, peeling potatoes, etc. Much of the mess equipment had to be drawn by horses or mules. Here, as an example, is a horse-drawn field kitchen during maneuvers, being pulled behind a caisson upon which rode part of the kitchen detail. The rest walked behind ready to set up for the preparation of meals as soon as mess area was reached. Note the tall stovepipe above the rolling stove. The units carried all the cooking utensils and even fuel. The old saying that "An army travels on its stomach" — meaning good food and plenty of it is vital to an army's success — must have been hard to live up to, even when tried by American Doughboys.

"Roll The Wagons!"

Before the days of mechanized equipment such as personnel carriers, troop trucks, jeeps, and other modern equipment for the movement of troops, weapons and supplies, the reliable but occasionally temperamental army mule was the main source of mobile power. Shown in this unusual photo of World War I vintage is a massed column of mule-drawn troop wagons. There are over 250 wagons drawn by over 1,000 of those long-eared power plants in this one massing of wagons. The feeding of so many animals was in itself a major supply problem, to say nothing of the supplies for the personnel involved. In spite of the army mule's occasional cussedness many old-time army men regret the passing of the animal, so long a colorful and essential part of the American Army's vigorous history.

Ammunition Train Encampment

In World War I, when any kind of transportation depot or encampment was established, such as the encampment of this ammunition train near Essey, Meurthe et Moselle, France, there also had to be provision for the animals. In this photo you can see the long line of mules tethered to the picket lines, caisson wheels or anything handy. (The long line of covered guns and caissons appear to be French 75 mm. pieces.) Note also the narrow-gauge railway tracks in the foreground and the pup tents pitched along the slope of the hill in the background. Mules and other draft animals contributed plenty of muscle to the Allied war effort, all for a few bales of hay.

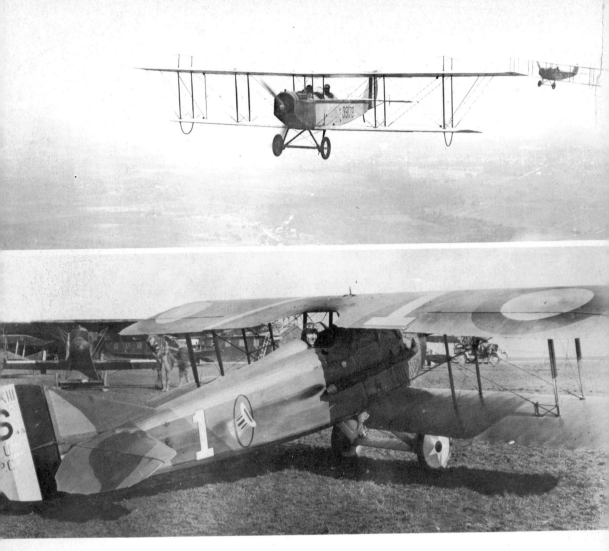

Flying Fighting Gear

Although this book is not about aircraft it seems only fitting to include these two photos. One of the most important contributions to the Allied cause was our pilot training program, and the mainstay of that program was the Curtiss JN-4D (top), known as the "Jenny" from the initials J N. In 1917 there were 65 officers and 1,120 enlisted men in the U. S. Air Service. By the end of the war it had more than 14,000 officers and 125,000 men. Most of our aircraft-building effort at first was aimed at pilot training and training aircraft. Our pilots completed their training overseas in already combat-proven French and English aircraft. Below, our top ace of World War I, Lieutenant (then) Edward V. Rickenbacker, later to become the famous Captain "Eddie" Rickenbacker, with a record of twenty-one enemy aircraft and four balloons to his credit and holder of the Congressional Medal of Honor (first such medal awarded for air activity). He is shown in his famous French SPAD XIII fighter plane with his "hat in the ring" insignia.

Aerial Bombs of World War I

In this day and age of the atomic and hydrogen bombs, these aerial bombs of the first World War seem pretty primitive. They were, but the results were deadly and devastating, for defenses against them were primitive, too. Left to right, they are the 155 mm., the 115 mm., the 90 mm. and the 75 mm. Most of these were dropped from wing racks rather than from internal bomb bays, for the day of the huge "block buster" bombs — bombs which were carried in the bomb bays of World War II aircraft — had not arrived. Today one aircraft can carry more destructive power than all the bombs dropped by all the aircraft of World War I and World War II combined.

The War's Last Shot

This battered and mud-caked French 155 mm. howitzer in use by American artillery-men of the 11th Field Artillery unit, serial number 3125, fired the last shot of World War I on November 11, 1918. Its location for this final historic shot was in the Bois de le Haie, on the Laneuville sur Meuse Beauclair road, Meuse, France. It seems fitting that this gun should be the final photo in this book about the fighting gear of World War I. Photo shows First Lieutenant H. F. Phillips, hand on lanyard, who fired the last round of what the world hoped would be the last such war.